Viva Mexico!

The Fiestas

George Ancona

BENCHMARK BOOKS

MARSHALL CAVENDISH
NEW YORK

To Jim and Barbara Dunlop

Gracias to the people who helped me with this project: Victor *(Chícharo)* Carrasco
and his family in Veracruz, Gabriel Alatriste Montoto in Puebla, Benjamin Salazar and
Martha Carrasco Salazar, Jim Dunlop of Alla Books, Barbara Mauldin of the
Museum of International Folk Art.

Benchmark Books
Marshall Cavendish Corporation
99 White Plains Road
Tarrytown, New York 10591-9001
www.marshallcavendish.com
Copyright © 2002 by George Ancona

Library of Congress Cataloging-in-Publication Data
Ancona, George.
The fiestas / by George Ancona.
p.   cm. — (Viva Mexico!)
Includes index.
ISBN 0-7614-1327-8
1. Festivals—Mexico—Juvenile literature. 2. Mexico—Social life and
customs—Juvenile literature. [1. Festivals—Mexico. 2. Holidays—
Mexico. 3. Mexico—Social life and customs.] I. Title. II. Series.
GT4814.A2A53 2001   394.26972—dc21   00-065080

Printed in Hong Kong
6 4 2 5 3 1

Contents

Fiestas

As they say in Mexico, *Los Mexicanos son muy festejeros*—Mexicans are very festive. If you look at a Mexican calendar, you will see that a fiesta, or festival, takes place almost every day of the year in some city, town, or village. There are religious holidays, saints' days, patriotic holidays, and regional fairs. The festivals vary, but most of them use the same elements: fireworks, music, dance, processions, costumes, piñatas, and, of course, food.

For weeks before a fiesta each town prepares by stringing sheets of *papel picado* (paper cutouts) above the streets and plazas. People of all ages practice for the days and nights of music, dance, theater, and, in many cases, mischief-making.

So much work goes into preparing for a brief moment in time. Piñatas are lovingly made, then broken with a stick to release their contents of fruit and candy. *Toritos* (little bulls) are loaded with fireworks and exploded, leaving only a cloud of smoke behind.

Fireworks

The highlights of any fiesta are the fireworks. The tradition came from China, where gunpowder was invented. The Spanish brought fireworks from their Asian colonies to New Spain. Today, they are part of almost every fiesta in Mexico.

The town of Tultepec is famous for its fireworks makers, or *pirotécnicos*. Each neighborhood tries to outdo the other by building the best and biggest *toritos*. These are the bamboo and papier-mâché bulls that carry the fireworks. On the first afternoon of a fiesta, a parade of bulls winds its way to the *zócalo*, the central plaza of the town. Children and teenagers hold small *toritos* on their heads, and teams of men carry the giant bulls.

By the time the parade reaches the *zócalo*, night has fallen. The fireworks begin. The small *toritos* are lit first, and crowds of boys run to tease the boy carrying the exploding bull. He, in turn, whirls around to chase them. The spinning wheels on the *torito* shoot ground-spinners to the pavement, which wiggle under the leaping feet of the crowd. The more cautious people stand in the background to enjoy the wildness. Smoke and deafening explosions fill the plaza. *Torito* after *torito* is burned, until the big ones are ignited and pulled around the plaza to the cheers of the crowd.

Another form of fireworks is the *castillo*, or castle. A *castillo* is a forty-foot (12m) tall framework made of wood. Wheels and paper figures attached to the sides and top hold rockets.

When all is ready, the master *pirotécnico* lights the fuse. Suddenly a flame shoots up to the first wheel, which begins to spin and whistle. The flickering fuse moves up the castle, igniting wheel after wheel until it reaches the top. Clouds of colored smoke billow out as rockets screech and explode high above the town.

Once a year, in Tultepec, there is a competition to see who can make the most spectacular *castillo*. Clusters of rockets fly up and fill the blackness with flowers of fire. The castles burn late into the night as the crowds cheer the ones they like best.

Music

Music—a flute and drum, a marching band, or *mariachis*—is part of every fiesta. Bands wind their way through the streets to announce the beginning of the celebration. Each region of Mexico has its own kind of music.

In rural areas, people use percussive and wind instruments such as drums, rattles, and flutes. In towns, the influence of Spanish, French, and German music can be heard in the sound of brass and stringed instruments.

During the French occupation of Mexico from 1863 until 1867, musicians who played for weddings were called *mariachis*, from the French word for wedding. Today, *mariachis* use guitars, violins, and trumpets to play and sing the traditional songs of Mexico.

Dance

And whenever there is music, there is dance. It is with pride that men and women and boys and girls perform the traditional dances of Mexico and Latin America.

The national dance is called the *jarabe tapatío* (Mexican hat dance). Women usually dress as *China poblanas*, after the legend of a Chinese princess who was kidnapped and brought to Mexico. Men dress as *charros*, Mexican horsemen. They dance fast, heel-stomping steps, which come from Spain.

On the east coast, musicians play and sing *huapangos* with guitars and a harp. They accompany dancers who perform dances like *la bamba*. The dance begins as the man holds one end of the sash wrapped around his partner's waist. The woman spins around to unwind the sash, which the dancers then place on the floor and tie into a bow with their feet.

In the south, on the Yucatan Peninsula, the music of the *jarana* accompanies dancers, who balance bottles or glasses or even trays of glasses on their heads.

In the north, European polkas have blended with Mexican rhythms to create a style of music called *norteño*, from the north. An accordion joins the guitar and the voices to create a special sound.

Carnaval

Carnaval, or carnival, is a springtime celebration held in many countries of Europe and Latin America. It is a time for frolic and fun before the solemn days of Lent, which end on Easter. It usually begins the Friday before the Christian holy day of Ash Wednesday. Mexicans often celebrate *carnaval* by dressing in costumes and masks.

In Veracruz the first night of *carnaval* begins with the burning of *el mal humor* (bad humor). Crowds gather in the main plaza where a giant puppet made of bamboo strips and tissue paper stands. The puppet is the likeness of a person with a bad reputation.

Tonight is the night that *mal humor* will be burned to make way for the good. As soon as the puppet disappears in flames, *carnaval* begins. Masked people enter the plaza dancing. Couples, young and old, join in the *danzón*, a traditional dance brought from Cuba, and dance into the night under the stars.

19

For five days and nights the streets are filled with dancers, bands, and bystanders who join in the fun. Each town celebrates *carnaval* in its own way. The first day, groups of children march by in costumes. They are followed by parades of stilt walkers, clowns, and many different bands. As one dancer said, "If we don't go out to *carnaval*, who will give joy to the children?"

In Tlaxcala, groups of men dance down the streets, dressed in the town's unique costumes and masks, a tradition that goes back hundreds of years.

Carnaval began in Egypt, where barges filled with masked and costumed dancers would float down the Nile River. After invading Egypt, the Romans returned to Italy and introduced the festival of *carnaval* to Europe. In pre-Christian times it represented the end of winter. Many centuries later the Spanish brought it to New Spain.

During the sixteenth century, wealthy whites celebrated *carnaval* as they had in Europe. Native people watched them and began to imitate the fancy dress of the upper class. They wore white masks with blue eyes. The men danced in sequined capes and hats with huge colored feathers. The tradition continues to this day.

One group of masked dancers is called *los catrines*, the dandies. They dress in top hats and black suits with tails and carry open umbrellas. With young women as partners, they dance formal European dances.

Originally, women were not permitted to participate in *carnaval*. So men would dress up in women's clothes to do the couples' dances. This proved to be so much fun that many groups continue the tradition today.

Historic Battles

The town of Huejotzingo has its own way of celebrating *carnaval.* The entire town takes part in the reenactment of the battle between the Mexicans and the French on May 5, 1862. (The anniversary of this battle is also a national holiday called *Cinco de Mayo.*)

The heroes of the battle were the Zacapoaxtlas, the Indians who used guerrilla warfare to win a temporary victory over the French. The invading French troops included *Turcos* from Turkey and *Zouaves* from Algeria. Both *carnaval* armies wear masks and carry muzzle-loading rifles, which fire gunpowder and fill the plaza with smoke. The bands play, and the soldiers dance. It is a noisy and wild fiesta.

Folk Plays

As in many towns, during the feast day of Tepoztlán the battle between the Moors and the Christians (*Moros y Cristianos*) is brought to life. The Moors ruled Spain for eight hundred years. The play celebrates the defeat of the Moors in 1492 by the army of the Catholic king Ferdinand and queen Isabella. For the first time in history, Spain was united under Christian rule.

The men dressed in red are the Moors, while the Christians wear blue. A narrator recites the history for the audience as the two armies act out the battle and the surrender.

Los Voladores

Long before the coming of the Spanish, people on Mexico's east coast performed a ritual to honor the gods of the four directions, north, south, east, and west. It was their way of asking for rain and other help from nature. Today, *los voladores* (the birdmen or flyers) come from the town of Papantla and perform during festivals.

 Five men, one playing a flute and a small drum, circle the base of a one hundred-foot (30m) pole. They are dressed in colorful costumes and caps with colored tassels. One by one, they climb up to a rotating platform at the top of the pole. While the musician sits and plays on the platform, the four men tie ropes to the pole and wrap them around it. Then, after tying the end of their ropes around their waists, they drop off the platform backward. Like birds, they spin around the pole upside down with their arms outstretched. Slowly the unwinding ropes lower them closer and closer to the ground. Just before they reach the earth, they turn right side up and nimbly jog to a halt.

Saints' Days

When the Spanish landed on the shores of what is today Mexico, they brought the Catholic religion with its calendar of saints' days. As cities were built, people adopted saints and built churches in their honor. One day a year is set aside in every town to celebrate its patron saint. But the fiestas often go on for many days.

On the saint's day of the town of Tultepec, the church is decorated. The front is covered with floral decorations that surround the picture of San Juan de Dios, their patron saint. Around the church garden, a carpet of colored sawdust is sprinkled on stencils to create beautiful designs. Led by a priest, worshipers carry the statue of their patron saint over the carpet. After they have passed, only smudges of colored sawdust remain.

Holidays

Día de la Bandera (Flag Day). On February 24, Mexico is
ablaze in red, white, and green, the colors of the Mexican flag.
The red represents human life; the white, the purity of human
beings united with God; and the green, nature. Parents crowd
into school playgrounds to watch their children reenact the
drama of their country's history.

   After raising and saluting the flag, students recite poems
and deliver speeches about the flag and what it represents.
Then the pageant begins. Students are dressed in costumes
of the nation's heroes. The boys wear wigs, beards, and
mustaches, acting the part of those who led their people
during pre-Colombian times through its revolutions for
independence and its battles against foreign invaders.

Cinco de Mayo. *Cinco de Mayo,* or the Fifth of May, is the day Mexico celebrates its 1862 victory over the French. This is a patriotic holiday celebrated with parades and sporting events throughout the country. In Puebla, near

where the battle against the French was fought, thousands
of students, teachers, nurses, bands, and soldiers march in
the parade. Cheers fill the air when the descendants of the
Zacapoaxtlas, the Indians who defeated the French, march by.

El Día del Charro (Day of the Horsemen). On September 14, Mexico celebrates *El Día del Charro* in honor of Mexican horsemen. The day begins with parades of *charros* and *charras*, men and women riders. They all wear sombreros, traditional wide-brimmed hats. Men wear elegant embroidered pants and jackets. Their leather saddles, silver stirrups, and bridles are decorated with elaborate designs. Women wear bright ruffled dresses.

38

After the parade, the riders assemble in the *lienzo*, an arena where the *charreada* will take place. In the Mexican-style rodeo, *charros* pit their skills against each other. They compete at cattle roping and horseback riding.

During an intermission, *mariachis* play while a group of *escaramuzas* enters the ring. These are young women who ride sidesaddle on sprightly horses. They perform an equestrian ballet and then gallop away to the thunderous applause of the spectators.

Independence Day. On September 16, 1810, Father Miguel Hidalgo y Costilla, the priest of the town of Dolores, rang the bells of the church and shouted his *Grito de Dolores* (Cry of Dolores). This was the beginning of the ten-year revolution for the independence of Mexico. The holiday begins the night before at eleven o'clock. In every plaza throughout Mexico a bell is rung and the *Grito* is shouted by mayors, governors, and the president. Thousands of people gather to cry out: "*¡Viva México! ¡Viva México! ¡Viva México!*" (Long Live Mexico!)

And so the festivities begin. There are fireworks, parades, and dances. In the town of Guanajuato, *estudiantinas*, groups of university students in medieval costumes, sing and dance for the crowds who follow them through the streets.

Día de los Muertos. On November 2, Mexico celebrates
Día de los Muertos, or the Day of the Dead. This is a holiday
when families remember their dead relatives by decorating
their graves with flowers and candles and their favorite
foods. This respect for the dead has been a tradition among
the people of Mexico since early times.

At home, the family builds and decorates an altar of offerings in memory of their dead relatives. The table is covered with food, flowers, sugar skulls and *pan de muertos*, "bread of the dead." Neighbors, friends, and relatives arrive with baskets of food to place on the altar. They eat and then take food to the next house.

In the evening, families gather in the town cemetery. As the flames of the candles flutter in the breeze, the adults pray, sing, or visit with neighbors, while the children play among the tombstones. As the night turns dark and cool, the sleepy children are gathered up and taken home, where they drink hot chocolate, eat *pan de muertos*, and then curl up to sleep.

On this day, the living have kept the spirits of the dead alive. Loved ones are never forgotten. This holiday, like the others throughout the year, leaves fond memories of the friendship and love that bring people together. After all, that's what fiestas are all about.

Calendar

There are far too many fiestas to describe in one book. Here are just a few celebrated throughout the Mexican year:

January 6 **Día de Reyes** (Three Kings Day)
Children receive their Christmas gifts. A *rosca*, or pastry, with a tiny doll in it is served. The person who finds the doll hosts a *tamalada*, a tamale dinner, on February 2.

February 2 **La Candelaria** (Candlemass)
The day Jesus was presented at the temple in Jerusalem. The host of the dinner serves tamales. *El Niño Santo*, a doll representing the Holy Child, is placed on the table.

March / April **Semana Santa** (Holy Week)
The last week of Lent, which ends with Good Friday and Easter. *Cascarones*, eggs filled with confetti, are broken on the heads of friends.

May 15 **Fiesta de San Isidro**
A sowing festival, in which seeds and animals are blessed. Oxen are decorated with flowers and paraded through the towns. Folk plays and dances are performed, and the blessing of the oxen takes place.

May / June **Las Mulitas** (Little Mules)
Little mules made of cornhusks carry the first fruits and flowers of spring. Voladores perform, and there are dances, bullfights, and parades of children dressed in costumes.

September 13 **Día de los Niños Heroes** (Day of the Boy Heroes)
A remembrance of the six cadets who leaped to their deaths from the Castle of Chapultepec rather than be captured by American invaders.

December 3-12 **Día de Nuestra Señora de Guadalupe** (Day of the Virgin of Guadalupe)
This day honors Mexico's patron saint. Pilgrimages are made, and bullfights, horse races, and pageants are held.

December 15-31 **Navidad** (Christmas)
A Christian holiday. *Las Posadas*, a reenactment of Mary and Joseph searching for lodging in Bethlehem, goes on for nine nights. Piñatas are broken.

December 31 New Year's Eve
A late dinner with a dessert of twelve grapes. At midnight, diners try to eat one grape at each stroke of the clock. Those who succeed will have good luck in the New Year.

Glossary

Here are the Spanish words and place names in this book.

carnaval: carnival
castillo: castle
catrín: dandy
charreada: Mexican rodeo
charro, charra: horseman, horse-
woman
China Poblana: dress of Chinese
woman from Puebla
cristiano: Christian
danzón: Cuban music and dance
escaramuza: equestrian perfor-
mance by women
estudiantinas: group of university
student musicians
festejero: festive person
grito: shout
huapango: dance of Veracruz
Huejotzingo: city in the state of
Puebla

humor: humor
jarabe tapatío: Mexican hat dance
jarana: dance from Yucatan
la bamba: dance from Veracruz
lienzo: arena for a *charreada*
mariachi: musician
moro: Moor
muerto: dead
norteño: music from the north
pan: bread
pirotécnico: fireworks maker
Tepoztlán: town in the state of
Morelos
torito: little bull
¡Viva México! Long Live Mexico!
voladores: birdmen, flyers
Zacapoaxtlas: Indians from
Zacatecas
zócalo: main square

Find Out More

Ancona, George. *Fiesta Fireworks.* New York: Lothrop, Lee & Shepard
Books, 1998.
——————. *Pablo Remembers: The Fiesta of the Day of the Dead.* New
York: Lothrop, Lee & Shepard Books, 1993.
——————. *The Piñata Maker/El Piñatero.* San Diego: Harcourt Brace,
1994.
Harris, Zoe and Suzanne Williams. *Piñatas & Smiling Skeletons:
Celebrating Mexican Festivals.* Berkeley, California: Pacific View Press,
1998.
Illsley, Linda. *Mexico.* New York: Raintree Steck-Vaughn, 1999.
Silverthorne, Elizabeth. *Fiesta! Mexico's Great Celebrations.* Brookfield,
Connecticut: Millbrook Press, 1992.

Index

Page numbers for illustrations are in **boldface**

About the Author

George Ancona considers his work a celebration of what he sees, the people he meets, and the moments they spend together. Music is a call to dance and to photograph. He usually joins in the fiesta. His childhood memories of growing up in Brooklyn are still alive. He remembers being taken to fiestas and falling asleep stretched across two chairs while watching his parents dance to the music of Mexico. With this book he shares those memories.